# I WANT TO BE A
# VET

**By Joanna Brundle**

# BookLife
## PUBLISHING

©2020
BookLife Publishing Ltd.
King's Lynn
Norfolk PE30 4LS

A catalogue record for this
book is available from the
British Library.

ISBN: 978-1-78637-956-6

**Written by:**
Joanna Brundle

**Edited by:**
William Anthony

**Designed by:**
Lydia Williams

## PHOTO CREDITS:

Images are courtesy of Shutterstock.com.
With thanks to Getty Images, Thinkstock Photo and iStockphoto.

Front Cover – Stokket, photomaster, 4 PM production, Life In Pixels, Korrapon Karapan, Africa Studio, Fesus Robert
2 – Syda Productions. 3 – Tom Wang. 4 – Alfazet Chronicles, hedgehog94, Gaidamashchuk. 5 – PRESSLAB. 6 – Dusan Petkovic.
7 – YAKOBCHUK VIACHESLAV. 8 – Klymenok, Olena. 9 – Sakan.p. 10 – Kachalkina Veronika, ChameleonsEye. 11 – DuxX, Alberto
Menendez, Cervero. 12 – Monkey Business Images, Jose Luis Carrascosa. 13 – Monkey Business Images. 14 – David Prado Perucha.
15 – nimon. 16&17 – Tyler Olson, 135pixels, Sergey Mikheev, frantic00, Kukota, didesign021. 18 – Ivonne Wierink. 19 – Jan Stria.
20 – Mary Ann McDonald, ChameleonsEye. 21 – Michalakis Ppalis, tropicdreams. 22 – Oleh Dovhan, Gaidamashchuk, KatePilko,
AVA Bitter, MoonRock, Shanvood, Rvector, KittyVector. 23 – Mascha Tace, paradesign, Victor Z, Ira Yapanda, Vector Up. Vector bone –
HitToon. Vector paw print – VectorPlotnikoff.

# CONTENTS

Words that look like <u>this</u> can be found in the glossary on page 24.

# HELLO, I'M VIREN!

Hello, I'm Viren! When I grow up, I want to be a vet. You could be one too! Let's find out what this job will be like.

I love animals. I've got a rabbit called Rosie. Do you have any pets?

I want to be a vet so that I can help animals who are sick. I want to make them better so that they can live happy, healthy lives with their owners.

There are animals all around the world who need help from vets.

# WHAT WILL I DO?

Vaccinations stop animals from getting serious diseases.

I will look after sick animals. These will include small pets, such as cats, and large farm and zoo animals.

I will give them the right treatments and medicines to make them better. I will also give vaccinations.

I will carry out operations and use x-rays to check for broken bones. Sometimes, I will treat animals that need emergency care.

I will give owners advice about a pet's food and exercise.

Vets have to be animal dentists too.

7

# HOW WILL I HELP PEOPLE?

Emergencies can happen at any time. Vets sometimes have to work through the night and at weekends.

My pet is like a member of my family. I feel upset if she is sick. Vets help us by doing everything they can to help our pets get better.

Dairy and <u>livestock</u> farmers earn money from their animals. Vets help farmers by keeping their animals healthy. Some vets check that food that comes from animals is being made safely.

Vets are often called to farms and zoos to help animals give birth.

# WHERE WILL I WORK?

Some vets work at animal clinics or hospitals, but vets work in lots of other places too. I might work at an animal rescue centre, a wildlife park or a centre for sea creatures.

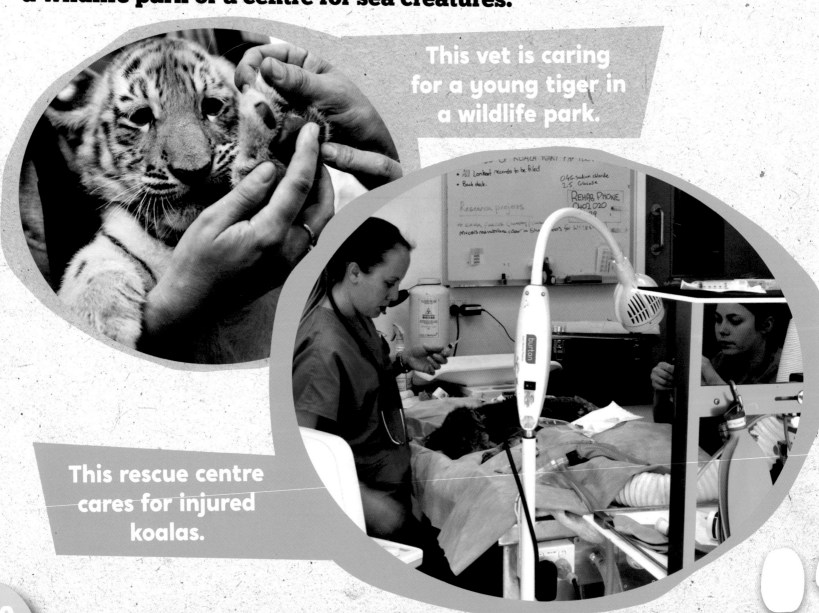

This vet is caring for a young tiger in a wildlife park.

This rescue centre cares for injured koalas.

Stable

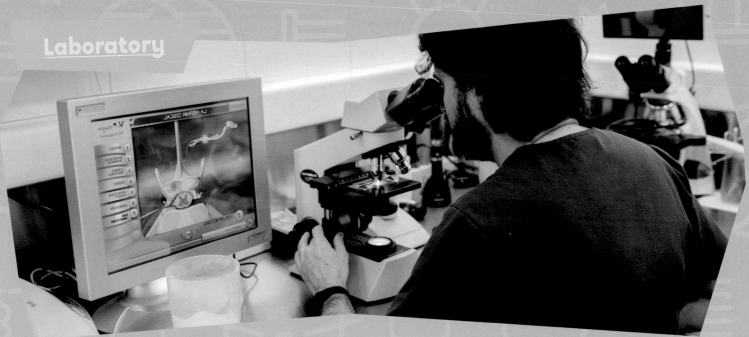

Laboratory

I love horses, so I might work at a stable. I might also choose to work in a laboratory, finding out more about animal diseases and how we can treat them.

# CAN I LOOK AROUND AN ANIMAL CLINIC?

Inside the clinic, there is a reception area for checking in and a waiting area.

Animals are examined in a room like this.

There are scales in the examination room for checking an animal's weight.

Further inside, there is an x-ray area and an <u>operating theatre</u>.
After an operation, an animal is cared for until it is ready to go home.

The clinic must be kept very clean to stop <u>infection</u>.

13

# WHAT WILL I WEAR?

I might wear scrubs. These are shirts and trousers that are loose-fitting to help me move around easily. Some vets wear normal clothes, with a white coat over the top.

Scrubs

Vets need clothes that can be cleaned easily.

14

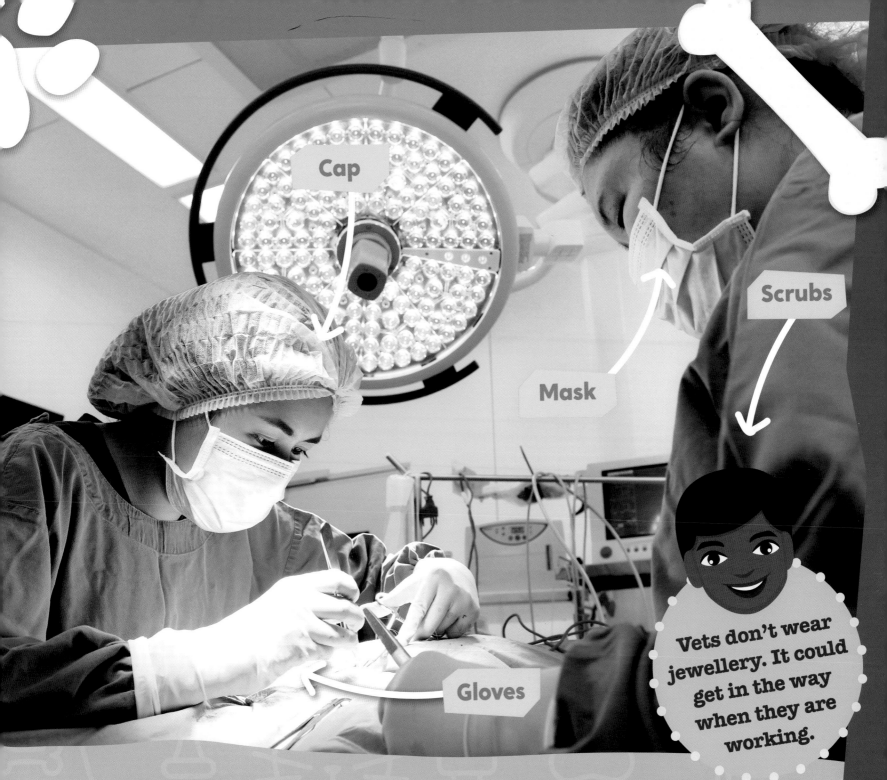

Cap

Scrubs

Mask

Gloves

Vets don't wear jewellery. It could get in the way when they are working.

I will always wear gloves when I am examining or treating an animal. In the operating theatre, I will also wear a mask over my nose and mouth and a cap to cover my hair.

# WHAT EQUIPMENT WILL I USE?

Let's have a look at some of the equipment I might use.

**Stethoscope** – used to listen to an animal's heart or breathing

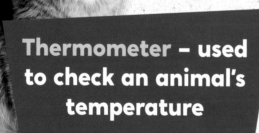

**Thermometer** – used to check an animal's temperature

**Otoscope** – used to look into an animal's ears to check for infection

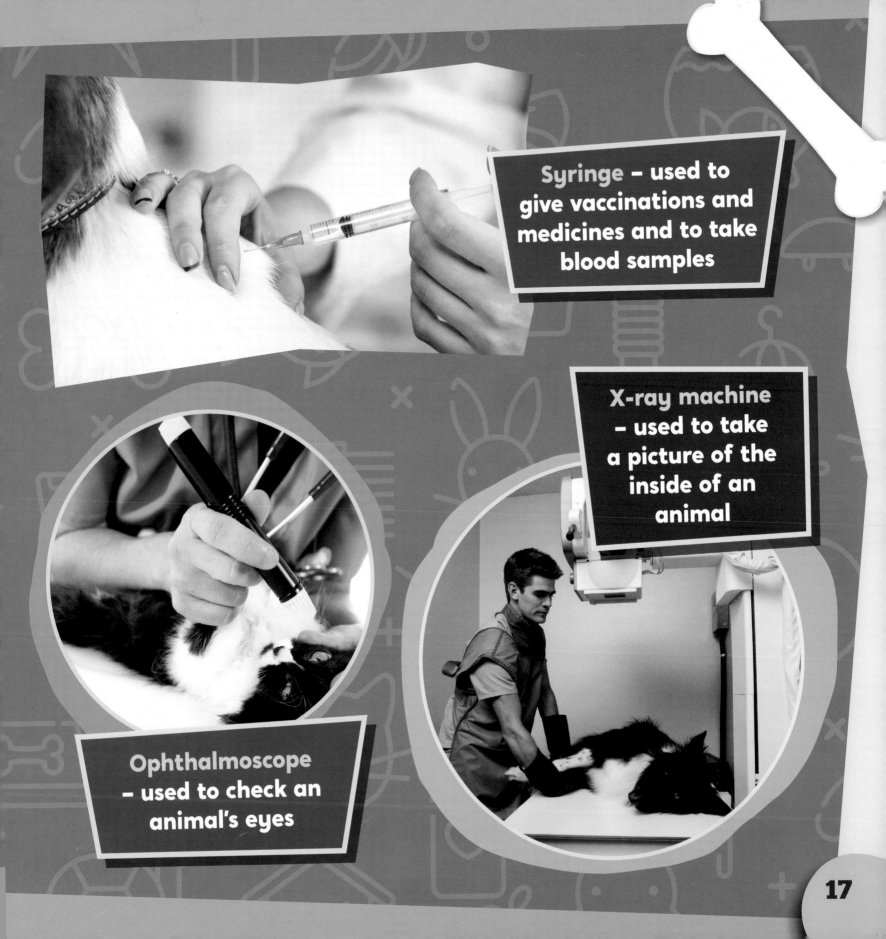

Syringe – used to give vaccinations and medicines and to take blood samples

X-ray machine – used to take a picture of the inside of an animal

Ophthalmoscope – used to check an animal's eyes

17

# HOW WILL I TRAVEL AROUND?

I may need to help an animal that can't be brought to the clinic by its owner. I might use a veterinary ambulance to visit an animal at home or bring it to the clinic.

The animal travels in this carrier to keep it safe on the journey.

Carrier

I might have to get out to places that are hard to reach, such as hill farms, whatever the weather. This means I may need a tough off-road vehicle.

Hill farm

19

# WHERE COULD I WORK AROUND THE WORLD?

I might work with an animal <u>conservation</u> or <u>welfare</u> charity. I could work with a mountain gorilla project in Uganda or a bear rescue centre in Asia.

AUSTRALIA ZOO
**WILDLIFE HOSPITAL**

**ENTRANCE THIS WAY**

I could work for a wildlife hospital like this one in Australia.

Some charities help animals injured in natural disasters such as floods or forest fires. Others work in countries such as India and Tanzania to vaccinate street dogs against <u>rabies</u>.

I might be a sea turtle vet, working in the US or the Indian Ocean.

# LET'S PRETEND

Let's work together. You be the vet. Let's pretend my rabbit Rosie has hurt her leg. Rosie cannot talk, so what questions will you need to ask me? Make a list.

When did you notice Rosie was acting differently?

What exactly was she doing that was different?

Have you noticed her trying not to use this leg?

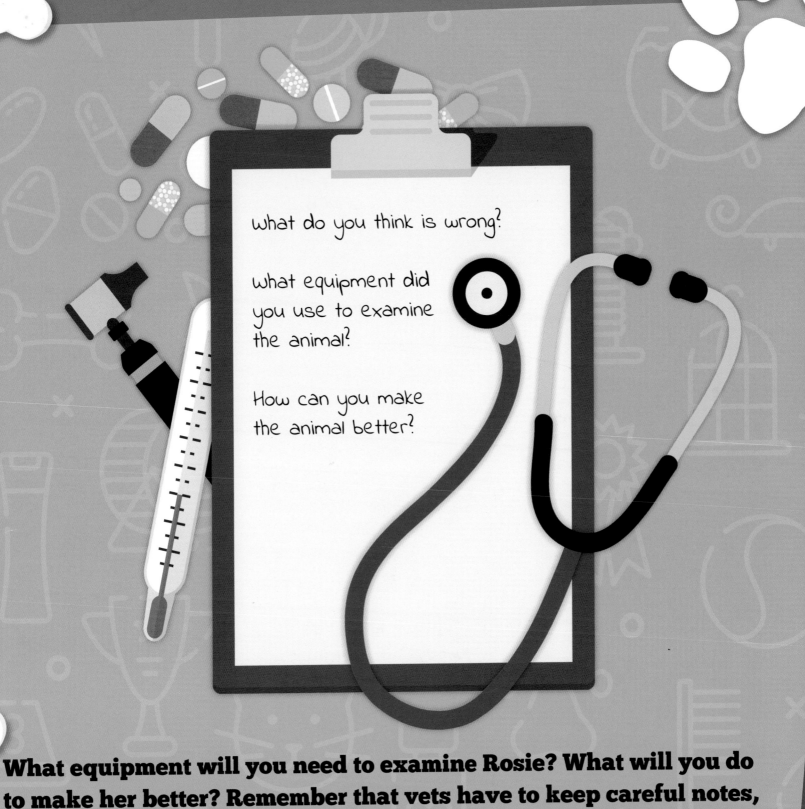

what do you think is wrong?

what equipment did you use to examine the animal?

How can you make the animal better?

What equipment will you need to examine Rosie? What will you do to make her better? Remember that vets have to keep careful notes, so write everything down.

# GLOSSARY

| | |
|---|---|
| CONSERVATION | looking after things found in nature, including wildlife |
| DISEASES | illnesses that cause harm to the health of an animal |
| EMERGENCY | a dangerous situation that requires action |
| INFECTION | illness caused by dirt or microbes getting into the body |
| LABORATORY | a room or building used by scientists to carry out experiments and research |
| LIVESTOCK | farm animals that are sold or used to make money |
| OPERATING THEATRE | a special room in a hospital or surgery in which operations are carried out |
| RABIES | a deadly disease that affects animals and can be passed on to people if they are bitten by an infected animal |
| VACCINATIONS | medicine that is injected into the body to help defend against disease and its spread |
| WELFARE | the well-being and health of an animal |
| X-RAYS | pictures taken by an x-ray machine that show the inside of an animal's body, particularly teeth and bones |

# INDEX